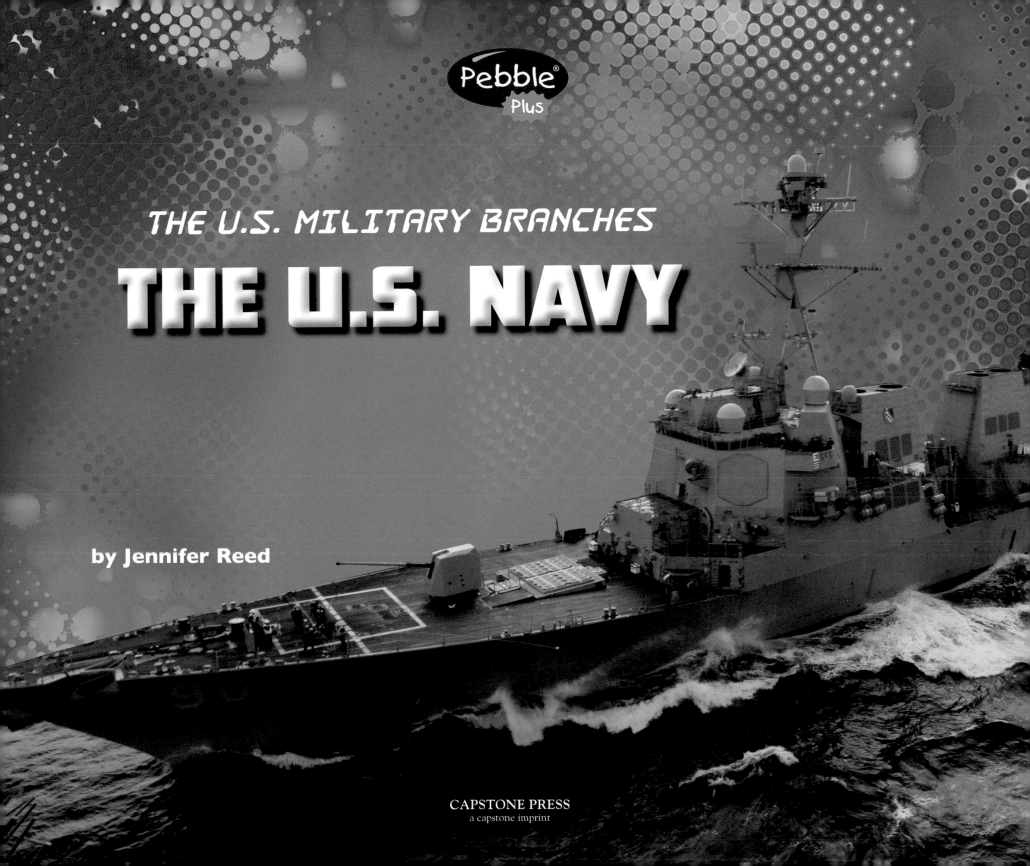

Pebble® Plus

THE U.S. MILITARY BRANCHES

THE U.S. NAVY

by Jennifer Reed

CAPSTONE PRESS
a capstone imprint

Pebble Plus is published by Capstone Press,
1710 Roe Crest Drive, North Mankato, Minnesota 56003
www.mycapstone.com

Library of Congress Cataloging-in-Publication Data
Names: Reed, Jennifer, 1967– author.
Title: The U.S. Navy / by Jennifer Reed.
Description: North Mankato, Minnesota : Capstone Press, [2018] | Series:
 Pebble plus. The U.S. military branches | Includes bibliographical
 references and index. | Audience: Grades K–3. | Audience: Ages 4–8.
Identifiers: LCCN 2016052800| ISBN 9781515767558 (library binding) |
ISBN 9781515767756 (pbk.) | ISBN 9781515767879 (ebook : .pdf)
Subjects: LCSH: United States. Navy—Juvenile literature.
Classification: LCC VA58.4 .R44 2018 | DDC 359.00973—dc23
LC record available at https://lccn.loc.gov/2016052800

Editorial Credits
Nikki Bruno Clapper, editor; Kayla Dohmen, designer; Jo Miller, media researcher;
Laura Manthe, production specialist

Image Credits
U.S. Navy photo by MCC Lucy M. Quinn, 19, MC2 Andrew Schneider, 17, MC2 Christian
Senyk, 5, 21, MC2 Gary A Prill, cover, MC3 Gregory A. Harden II, 7, MC3 Jasmine Sheard,
13, MC3 Ricardo J. Reyes, 15, PO3 Sean M. Castellano, 11, Seaman Weston A. Mohr, 1, MCSC
Andrew McKaskle, 9

Design Elements
Shutterstock: Andis Rea, Aqua, Evannovostro, Kolonko, Omelchenko

Note to Parents and Teachers

The U.S. Military Branches set supports national curriculum standards for science related
to science, technology, and society. This book describes and illustrates the U.S. Navy. The
images support early readers in understanding the text. The repetition of words and phrases
helps early readers learn new words. This book also introduces early readers to subject-
specific vocabulary words, which are defined in the Glossary section. Early readers may need
assistance to read some words and to use the Table of Contents, Glossary, Read More, Internet
Sites, Critical Thinking Questions, and Index sections of the book.

Printed in China.
010322F17

TABLE OF CONTENTS

Guards of the Sea

The Navy is a branch of the
United States Armed Forces.
The Navy guards the sea.
It helps protect the country.

Navy Jobs

All people in the Navy
are called sailors.
Some sailors are navigators.
They decide which way
ships will travel.

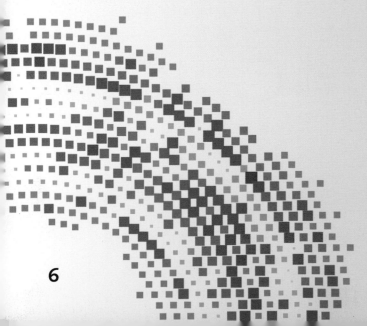

Navy divers work underwater.

Some divers rescue people.

Others fix ships.

Divers wear scuba gear.

Navy pilots fly
planes and helicopters.
Pilots deliver supplies
and fight battles. Some pilots
fly Seahawk helicopters.

The Navy has special forces.
Navy SEALs fight on land
and at sea. SEALs train
very hard. They learn
to jump out of planes.

Ships and Weapons

Aircraft carriers are
the largest Navy ships.
They are floating airports.
Planes and helicopters
take off and land from them.

Destroyers and cruisers are warships. They fight enemy ships and aircraft. They shoot large guns and missiles.

destroyer

17

Submarines travel underwater. They fire missiles called torpedoes. A Virginia-class submarine holds 132 sailors.

Sailing for the United States

Navy sailors do
dangerous jobs.
They stop attacks
from the sea. They risk
their lives for their country.

Glossary

Armed Forces—the whole military; the U.S. Armed Forces include the Army, Navy, Air Force, Marine Corps, and Coast Guard

branch—a part of a larger group

enemy—a person or group that wants to harm another person or group

guard—to protect a place

missile—an explosive weapon that is thrown or shot at a distant target

navigator—someone who decides the direction a vehicle should travel

rescue—to save someone who is in danger

scuba—swimming underwater with the help of special breathing equipment

submarine—a ship that can travel both on the surface of and under the water

torpedo—an underwater missile used to blow up a target

Read More

Callery, Sean. *Branches of the Military*. Discover More Readers. New York: Scholastic, 2015.

Marx, Mandy R. *Amazing U.S. Navy Facts*. Amazing Military Facts. North Mankato, Minn.: Capstone Press, 2017.

Murray, Julie. *United States Navy*. U.S. Armed Forces. Minneapolis: Abdo Kids, 2015.

Internet Sites

FactHound offers a safe, fun way to find Internet sites related to this book. All of the sites on FactHound have been researched by our staff.

Here's all you do:
Visit *www.facthound.com*
Type in this code: 9781515767558

Check out projects, games and lots more at
www.capstonekids.com

Critical Thinking Questions

1. What are two types of Navy ships? What do they do?

2. What does it mean to guard something? How do Navy sailors guard the sea?

3. What do Navy SEALs do?

Index